THE INDUS VALLEY CIVILISATION

Tim Cooke

W

Published in paperback in 2018 by
The Watts Publishing Group

For Brown Bear Books Ltd:
Managing Editor: Tim Cooke
Children's Publisher: Anne O'Daly
Editorial Director: Lindsey Lowe
Design Manager: Keith Davis
Designer and Illustrator: Supriya Sahai
Picture Manager: Sophie Mortimer

Concept development: Square and Circus/
Brown Bear Books Ltd

ISBN: 978 1 4451 6194 5

Printed in Malaysia

Franklin Watts
An imprint of
Hachette Children's Group
Part of the Watts Publishing Group
Carmelite House
50 Victoria Embankment
London EC4Y 0DZ

An Hachette UK company
www.hachette.co.uk
www.franklinwatts.co.uk

FSC
www.fsc.org
MIX
Paper from
responsible sources
FSC® C137506

CONTENTS

THE INDUS VALLEY CIVILISATION

Between about 3000 and 1800 BCE,
an ancient culture flourished in modern-day
Pakistan and northern India. By about 1300 BCE,
a combination of a drier climate and
the arrival of invaders had pushed the
Indus Valley people eastward.

TOWNS AND RIVERS

The civilisation covered around 1.3 million square kilometres along the River Indus. Most of the people lived in large towns. The most important were Harappa and Mohenjo Daro. Their ruins were rediscovered in the 1920s. Other important towns included Lothal, which was a port, and Chanu Daro.

The towns in the Indus Valley stood on the banks of rivers and streams. Most had populations of about 5,000 people, but the larger towns were home to up to 40,000 people. The towns were laid out with regular streets, brick buildings and indoor plumbing.

The ancient dock at the port of Lothal. From there, ships sailed as far as Africa and West Asia.

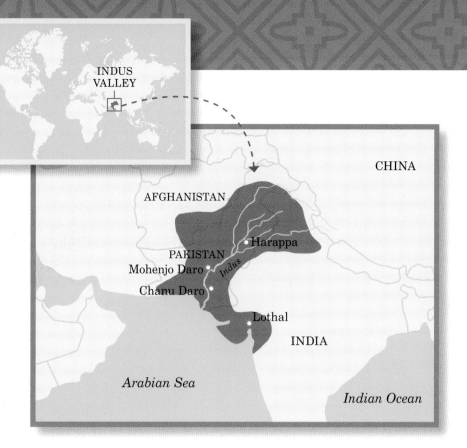

ARTEFACTS

Today, the Indus Valley civilisation is known mainly through the ruins of its cities and its artefacts. The things people made reveal information about their daily lives, such as what they ate or wore. Artworks depict the gods people worshipped, while weapons and armour tell us how they went to war. One of the best ways to understand the Indus Valley civilisation today is by studying the things people made.

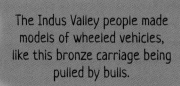

The Indus Valley people made models of wheeled vehicles, like this bronze carriage being pulled by bulls.

FARMING THE LAND

The Indus Valley civilisation was based on agriculture. The Indus and other rivers flooded every year, carrying silt across the land. This made the soil very fertile. Farmers grew crops to support the population in the towns.

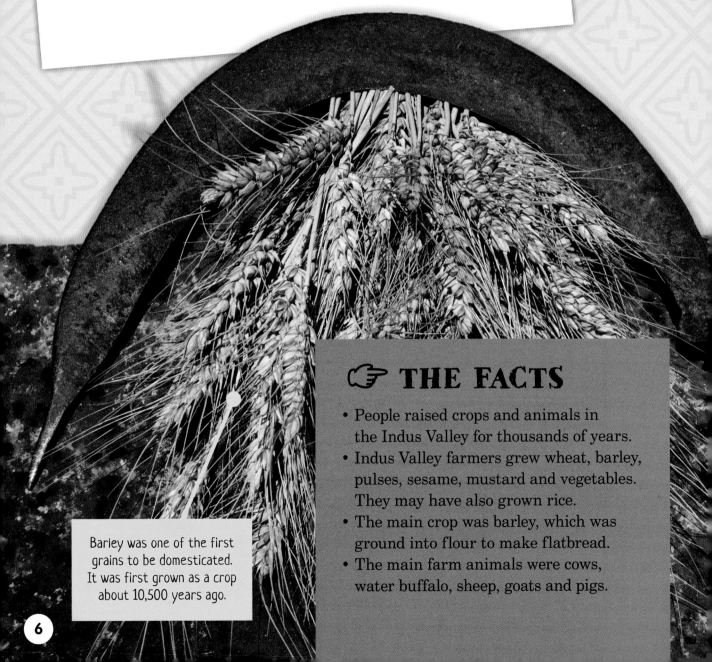

Barley was one of the first grains to be domesticated. It was first grown as a crop about 10,500 years ago.

☞ THE FACTS

- People raised crops and animals in the Indus Valley for thousands of years.
- Indus Valley farmers grew wheat, barley, pulses, sesame, mustard and vegetables. They may have also grown rice.
- The main crop was barley, which was ground into flour to make flatbread.
- The main farm animals were cows, water buffalo, sheep, goats and pigs.

PLATFORMS

Archaeologists uncovered 12 circular platforms in Harappa. The platforms are made from rings of regular-shaped bricks.

Each platform had four rings of bricks with a small hollow in the middle. The bricks were cemented in place using mud as mortar. The platforms are arranged in two rows, with about 6 metres between the rows. At one time, people thought the platforms had belonged to a public building. Now, most archaeologists think the platforms might have been used to thresh barley to release its grains.

Grain was ground between millstones to produce flour.

Barley was harvested by hand using hooked tools called sickles. Early sickles in the Indus Valley were often made from stone.

URBANISATION

Towns and cities appeared in the Indus Valley from about 3300 BCE. They were carefully planned, with different sections for various activities, such as shopping. The streets were laid out in a grid pattern. They had drains and sewerage systems to take away rubbish and wells for clean water. Some houses had indoor plumbing and bathrooms.

☞ THE FACTS

Historians think that towns emerged in the Indus Valley because of changes to the climate. The parts of the valley furthest from the rivers became drier, making farming there more difficult. So people started to settle in towns close to rivers and streams. Some towns had thick walls of mud and brick to protect them from attack by enemies. The walls also protected the towns from the regular flooding of the rivers.

The walls of this well in Mohenjo Daro were built higher as flooding filled the streets around it with silt.

BULLOCK CART

The development of wheeled transport happened by the third millennium BCE. This was one of the advances that made the growth of towns possible.

Wheeled carts made it easier to move crops and goods from the countryside to the towns. They allowed people to farm and trade on a larger scale. This clay model of a cart being pulled by a pair of bullocks was found in the ruins of Lothal. Models of different types of cart have been found, suggesting that people had different types of cart for different purposes.

This channel was part of the drainage system at Lothal.

The streets were laid out in a regular grid. This suggests that the growth of the city was planned.

This model of a bullock cart was made in Lothal in around 2700 BCE. It has lost its wheels.

TOWNS AND CITIES

Indus Valley towns had public buildings, such as baths and meeting halls. There were also granaries and wells. At Mohenjo Daro, the important buildings stood on a central mound known today as the Citadel.

PAKISTAN
Mohenjo Daro
Indus
INDIA

Archaeologists believe that some of the brick walls on the Citadel supported wooden buildings that have rotted away.

 **THE FACTS**

- Covered drains in the streets took away wastewater from the bathrooms in individual homes.
- Buildings had flat roofs, where people may have relaxed, prepared food and cooked.
- Mohenjo Daro had a central marketplace for trade.

- There were wells throughout the city. People used the water for drinking and cooking, and for keeping clean.
- Public buildings and workers' homes were built from regular bricks made from mud.

THE GREAT BATH

In 1926, archaeologists working on the Citadel at Mohenjo Daro discovered one of the oldest baths in the world.

The Great Bath is a water tank that measures about 12 by 7 metres, with a maximum depth of 2.4 metres. Two sets of stairs lead down into the tank on the north and south sides. The bottom and sides of the bath were lined with tightly fitting bricks. In order to make them more waterproof, the bricks were covered with a layer of natural tar, called bitumen. The bath was surrounded by a group of rooms. Experts think that the pool may have been used for rituals in which bathers symbolically cleaned themselves.

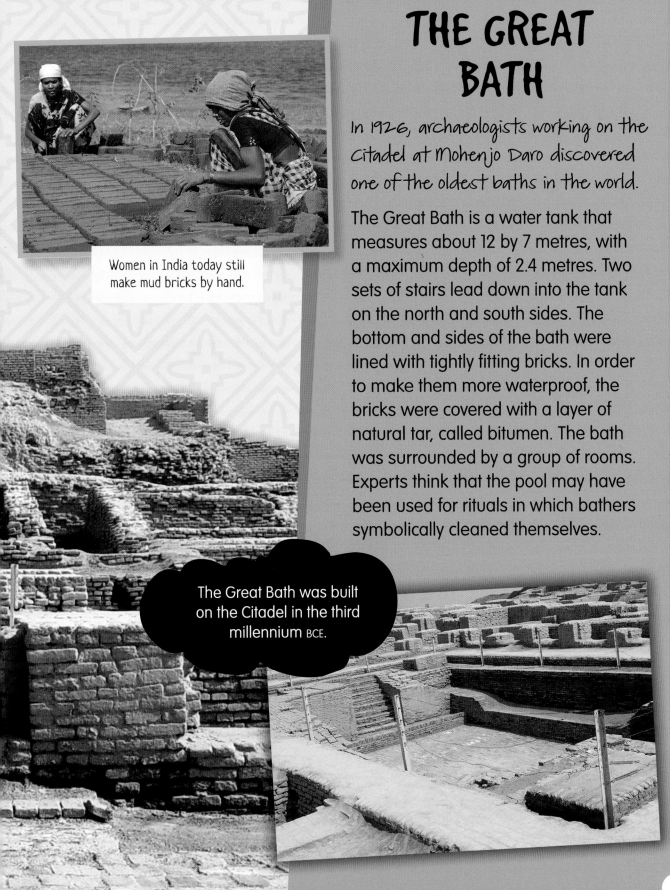

Women in India today still make mud bricks by hand.

The Great Bath was built on the Citadel in the third millennium BCE.

11

INDUS VALLEY SOCIETY

No one knows how society was organised in the Indus Valley, or what sort of rulers it had. Modern experts think the civilisation was highly organized. They think that it was probably governed from twin capitals based in the largest cities, Mohenjo Daro and Harappa.

☞ THE FACTS

- It is not clear whether the Indus Valley rulers were powerful kings or priests.
- There are no ruins of large palaces or temples, even in the largest cities.
- Wealthy people were buried with high-quality pottery, seals and metal objects. No burials seem to be so luxurious that they might have belonged to a royal family.
- Some experts argue that the society had no rulers and that everyone had a say in local goverment.
- Another theory is that there was one powerful ruler, or that each town or city had its own ruler.

This photo shows the ruins of Harappa from the air. No one knows who planned the regular layout of the streets.

PRIEST KING

This small carving in a soft stone called steatite was found in 1927.

It was found in the ruins of a small house in the lower city of Mohenjo Daro, where ordinary people lived. This statue is one of the only surviving portraits of someone from the Indus Valley civilisation. The man has been named the 'priest king' because of his solemn expression and his decorated headband and arm ornament. The cloak is decorated with three-lobed patterns called trefoils.

Indus Valley towns had large market areas, like this one in Dholavira.

The 'priest king' is only 17.7 centimetres tall. Despite the statue's name, there is no evidence that priests ruled Indus Valley towns.

POTTERY

Some of the most common artefacts found in Indus Valley settlements are pieces of pottery. Pottery was made from clay, then baked in kilns to harden it. Most towns had their own kiln and produced vases, jars and other containers.

☞ THE FACTS

The first pottery in the Indus Valley was made by coiling clay into bowl-like shapes and smoothing over the sides. The potter's wheel was being used in the Indus Valley by about 3500 BCE. Potters made bowls, dishes, cups and vases from red clay called terracotta. The style of pottery changed over time. This means that archaeologists can tell approximately when items of pottery they find in the Indus Valley were made.

TERRACOTTA

This piece of terracotta found at the settlement of Chanhudaro comes from the side of a deep vase.

The fragment shows the most common form of pottery decoration used in the Indus Valley. The clay was covered in a reddish layer called a slip, then painted with black flowers or geometrical shapes. Common designs included bands of black and shapes like fish scales. Some pots were more colourful reds, greens, blues and yellows.

This lipped vessel was found in the ruins of Harappa.

A modern potter's wheel is similar to those that were used in the Indus Valley. It spins at a regular speed to allow the potter to shape the clay.

The black design on this piece of pottery shows a humped bull with a number of birds.

SEALS AND WRITING

Archaeologists have found more than 3,500 seals in the Indus Valley towns. These seals were used to press shapes into clay, probably to create labels. The seals were engraved into steatite. They contain symbols that may be a type of writing.

Humped bulls like those that appeared on many seals are still used in South Asia to pull ploughs or for their meat.

👉 THE FACTS

The original design of a seal was carefully carved into a piece of soft stone. The stone seal was pressed into a small piece of damp clay to create a square with a copy of the design. Once the clay dried, the seal became like a hard, solid tag.

Some seals had holes in them, so they could be tied on to objects such as storage jars or sacks. Some seals may have been used to show who owned which goods. Officials might also have issued tags to show that the correct taxes had been paid on trade goods.

Indus writing usually appears in small groups of symbols. The longest known inscription has 14 symbols.

CLAY SEAL

This seal contains a detailed picture of a type of humped cow called a zebu. It was an important farm animal in the Indus Valley.

Zebus were used for their meat and their skins, and were used to pull carts and ploughs. Other seals depicted wild animals such as rhinoceroses and elephants. Alongside the zebu on this seal are symbols that experts think belong to a writing system. Indus Valley writing used about 400 picture symbols. No one has been able to work out what the signs mean.

The zebu was so important it may have been a religious symbol in the Indus Valley.

TRADE

The Indus Valley people traded with other civilisations. Goods from the Indus Valley have been found in the Persian Gulf, in modern-day Iraq and in Iran. Indus Valley artisans imported copper from Rajasthan in northern India, semi-precious stones from Central Asia and gold from southern India.

In this illustration, an Indus Valley trader uses a balance scale to check the weight of jewellery.

☞ THE FACTS

Trade was important in Indus Valley towns. Merchants lived in homes with workshops and stores attached. The towns traded with each other and with regions outside the Indus Valley which had valuable stone, such as lapis lazuli. A lot of trade was done by sea. Ships sailed from the harbour at Lothal to West Asia and Africa.

A trader bargains with a colleague over lapis lazuli. The valuable blue stone came from mines in what is now Afghanistan.

WEIGHTS AND SCALES

This balance scale and set of weights were found in the ruins of Harappa.

Similar sets of stone weights have been found throughout the Indus Valley. Each weight was twice as heavy as the next smallest. The smaller weights were most common. The weights are highly standardised everywhere in the Indus Valley. This suggests that the weights and measures used throughout the Indus Valley were set by a central authority. They were probably checked regularly to prevent dishonest trading.

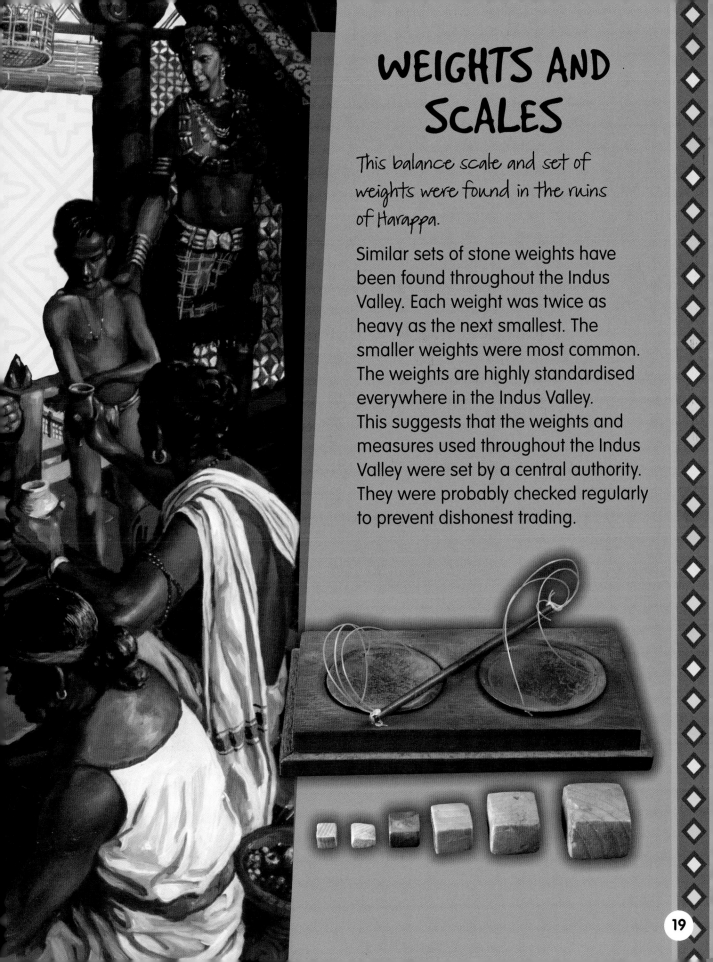

RELIGION

We know very little about the religion of the Indus Valley. Archaeologists have found figurines that may show fertility goddesses. Parts of the religion might have influenced the Indian religion Hinduism, which began about 300 years after the end of the Indus Valley civilisation.

This statue of a fertility goddess known as a Mother Goddess was found in Mohenjo Daro.

This modern statue shows the Hindu god Shiva. The Indus people may have worshipped an early form of the god.

GOD SEAL

This stone seal was found at Mohenjo Daro. It probably shows an Indus god.

The main image shows a seated figure with three faces. One face is looking forward, and the others look to each side. The figure has a headdress with horns on it and bangles on its arms. It is surrounded by pictures of animals. Horned gods were common in South Asia, so historians think this figure is a god. The Hindu god Shiva is also shown with three faces. Some experts think the figure on the seal is an early picture of Shiva.

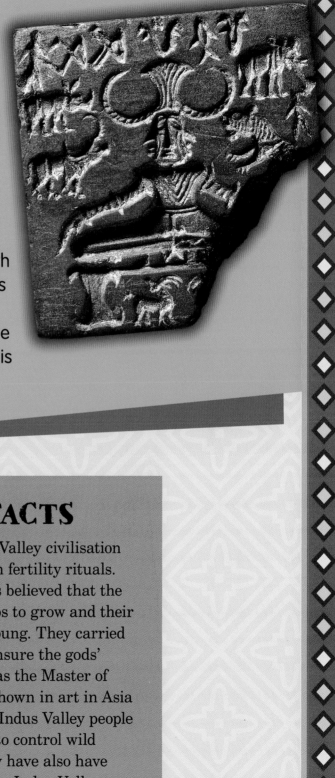

☞ THE FACTS

Religion in the Indus Valley civilisation was probably based on fertility rituals. Early farming peoples believed that the gods helped their crops to grow and their animals to produce young. They carried out rituals to try to ensure the gods' favour. A god known as the Master of Animals was widely shown in art in Asia at about the time the Indus Valley people lived. It was thought to control wild animals. The god may have also have been worshipped in the Indus Valley.

DAILY LIFE

People in the Indus Valley spent much of their time outside. Wealthy people had courtyards in their homes. Other people cooked, ate and relaxed on the flat roofs of their houses. People visited the market or the workshops that lined the streets. Some children probably went to school, where they were taught to read and write by priests or scribes.

A cross-section through a wall shows a man washing in his plumbed bathroom.

A reconstruction of an Indus Valley town in a museum in New Delhi, India.

☞ THE FACTS

The Indus Valley people liked to relax. They played musical instruments that looked like harps and made statues of dancing girls, so music may have been important. Children played games and had many toys, including toy animals that were pulled along on strings. People played games with dice that look like the ones we use today.

A potter displays pots and jars next to the wheel where he makes more articles to sell.

Traders use open-fronted workshops to sell their merchandise.

A woman checks the quality of cotton (see page 24) before buying it to make clothes.

BOARD GAME

This board and counters come from a game that was discovered at Harappa.

The game was probably played by moving counters around squares on the board. No one knows the rules. Because this is just a broken part of the board, we don't know how many squares there were or the number of counters. Archaeologists think that board games like this were played by adults rather than children. The players might have gambled on the results.

Some people think that Indus Valley board games, like this one, were like early versions of chess.

CLOTHES AND FASHION

The Indus Valley people were some of the first people in the world to weave cotton. Archaeologists have found the remains of cotton seeds at one settlement that date from 5000 BCE. Cotton was being woven in Harappa by 3300 BCE.

Traditional cotton weavers in India still use looms similar to those that would have been used in the Indus Valley.

👉 THE FACTS

- Cotton grew naturally in the Indus Valley.
- People learned how to separate its fine fibres and spin them into a long yarn.
- The yarn was woven in crisscross rows to make a light, soft cloth that was used for clothes and blankets.
- No Indus Valley cotton material has survived. It has all rotted away over the past 4,500 years.

NECKLACE

People in the Indus Valley wore jewellery with their clothing. They wore necklaces as well as brooches, amulets and bangles.

Cotton is made from the soft fibres of the cotton plant.

This necklace has long tubes of carnelian separated by darker balls of steatite (see page 13).

The weaver passes coloured threads through plain lengthwise threads to create a decorative pattern.

This necklace was found at Mohenjo Daro. It is made from a stone called carnelian. This was a reddish-brown stone that turned red when it was heated. Craftsmen used carnelian to make jewellery but they also used softer materials such as terracotta and faience. Other jewellery was made from metals, such as bronze, and shells. Some jewellery included lapis lazuli from Afghanistan (see page 18).

SHIVA AND PARVATI

Just as artefacts tell us a lot about cultures from the past, the stories people told also reveal what they thought about their world. Most ancient peoples told myths to explain their world. We don't know any stories from the Indus Valley people, but they may have included stories of a god, such as the Hindu god, Shiva.

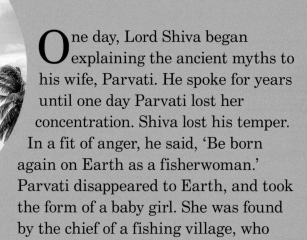

Hindus today worship Nandi in the form of a bull.

One day, Lord Shiva began explaining the ancient myths to his wife, Parvati. He spoke for years until one day Parvati lost her concentration. Shiva lost his temper. In a fit of anger, he said, 'Be born again on Earth as a fisherwoman.' Parvati disappeared to Earth, and took the form of a baby girl. She was found by the chief of a fishing village, who named her Parvati and brought her up as his own daughter. Years went by, and Parvati grew into a beautiful young woman.

Shiva missed his wife. His servant, Nandi the bull, could not bear to watch his master's suffering. Nandi urged Shiva to bring his wife back, but Shiva explained sadly that Parvati was now destined to marry a fisherman.

Nandi had other ideas. The next day he took the form of a large whale. He began to disturb the fishermen at sea, tearing their nets and sinking their boats. The fishermen complained to their chief, who announced, 'Whoever catches the whale can marry my daugher, Parvati.' Many young fishermen took their turn trying to catch the whale but failed. The chief then prayed to Shiva for help. Parvati prayed, too. Now Shiva took the form of a handsome young fisherman and went to the chief. He said, 'I am here to help you. I'll catch that whale and then marry your daughter Parvati.'

The young man set out to sea. Nandi transformed himself into the shape of the whale and allowed Shiva to catch him. The fishers were overjoyed. The chief arranged the marriage of the young man to Parvati. That was how Shiva got Parvati back as his beloved wife again.

TIMELINE OF THE INDUS VALLEY CIVILISATION

c.6000 BCE
First pottery made by the forerunners of the Indus Valley people.

c.4000 BCE
Farming settlements begin to grow up in the Indus Valley.

c.3500 BCE
The potter's wheel is introduced to the Indus Valley from the Middle East.

c.3300 BCE
The first towns and cities are built in the Indus Valley.

6000 BCE   4000 BCE   3000 BCE

c.5000 BCE
First evidence of religious practices in the Indus Valley.

c.3500 BCE
The first clay models of carts are made at Harappa.

c.3000 BCE
The towns of Harappa and Mohenjo Daro emerge as the centres of the Indus Valley.

c.3300 BCE
The first evidence of cotton weaving dates to this time.

c.2500 BCE
The Great Bath
is built at
Mohenjo Daro.

c.2600 BCE
Dozens of
towns and
cities are built
in the Indus
Valley region.

c.2000 BCE
The Indus Valley
begins to become
drier, due to
climate change.

| 2500 BCE | 2000 BCE | 1500 BCE |

c.2700 BCE
Traders
exchange goods
with Egypt,
Mesopotamia
(modern-day
Iraq) and the
Persian Gulf.

c.2000 BCE
The introduction
of wheeled carts
makes it easier
to trade.

c.1500 BCE
Nomads from
Central Asia
begin to move
into the Indus
Valley. They
push the Indus
people out.

c.2500 BCE
Earliest use of the
Indus Valley script.

GLOSSARY

amulet a piece of jewellery used as a good-luck charm

archaeologists people who study the past by examining the objects that remain

artefacts objects that are made by people, particularly in the past

artisans people who are skilled at making things by hand

bronze a metal made by mixing copper and tin

carnelian a dull-red semi-precious stone

citadel a fortress on high ground above a city

domesticated adapted wild plants and animals to be kept on farms

elevation height above the surrounding area

faience glazed pottery

fertile describes land able to produce large amounts of crops

fertility the ability of animals or plants to reproduce easily

flatbread a type of flat, thin bread

granaries buildings where grain is stored

gypsum a soft white mineral used to make plaster

inscriptions patterns or symbols scratched into a hard surface

kilns ovens for firing, or baking, pottery to harden it

merchants people who buy and sell large quanities of goods

nomads people who move around and have no fixed homes

rituals solemn ceremonies that follow a set series of actions

scribes people who copied out documents

sewerage a system of drains to take away waste water

silt fine sand or clay carried in rivers and deposited along their banks

steatite a soft stone made up of talc rock; also called soapstone

terracotta a type of red-brown clay used in building and to make pottery

thresh to separate grains from the stalks of a plant, uusually by hitting them with a rod or chain

trefoils designs with three rounded lobes, like leaves

urban related to towns and cities

urbanisation the process by which a culture comes to be dominated by towns and cities

FURTHER RESOURCES

Books

Explore the Indus Valley, Claudia Martin
(Wayland, 2017)

Parallel History The Ancient World, Alex Woolf
(Franklin Watts, 2017)

History Detective Investigates the Indus Valley, Claudia Martin
(Wayland, 2016)

Great Civilisations Indus Valley, Anita Ganeri
(Franklin Watts, 2014)

Websites

www.ancientindia.co.uk/indus/home_set.html
A British Museum site about the Indus Valley civilisation
with a story, an interactive map and a challenge
(click the links on the left).

www.bbc.co.uk/education/topics/zxn3r82
These pages from BBC Bitesize are intended
to help students with revision.

**www.bbc.co.uk/schools/primaryhistory/
indus_valley/land_of_the_indus/**
This BBC site has information about the Indus Valley civilisation
for primary school students.

www.theschoolrun.com/homework-help/the-indus-valley
Top 10 facts, a timeline, a gallery
and quiz questions to help students with homework projects
about the Indus Valley civilisation.

INDEX